Congressional Research Service

State Taxation of Internet Transactions

Steven Maguire

Specialist in Public Finance

November 1, 2011

Congressional Research Service

7-5700

www.crs.gov

R41853

CRS Report for Congress

Prepared for Members and Committees of Congress

c11173008

Summary

The United States Bureau of the Census estimated that $3.4 trillion worth of retail and wholesale transactions were conducted over the Internet in 2009. That amount was 16.8% of all U.S. shipments and sales in that year. Other estimates projected the 2011 so-called e-commerce volume at approximately $3.9 trillion. The volume of e-commerce is expected to increase and state and local governments are concerned because collection of sales taxes on these transactions is difficult to enforce.

Under current law, states cannot reach beyond their borders and compel out-of-state Internet vendors (those without nexus in the buyer's state) to collect the use tax owed by state residents and businesses. The Supreme Court ruled in 1967 that requiring remote vendors to collect the use tax would pose an undue burden on interstate commerce. Estimates put this lost tax revenue at approximately $11.4 billion in 2012.

Congress is involved because interstate commerce typically falls under the Commerce Clause of the Constitution. Opponents of remote vendor sales and use tax collection cite the complexity of the myriad state and local sales tax systems and the difficulty vendors would have in collecting and remitting use taxes. Proponents would like Congress to change the law and allow states to require out-of-state vendors without nexus to collect state use taxes. These proponents acknowledge that simplification and harmonization of state tax systems are likely prerequisites for Congress to consider approval of increased collection authority for states.

A number of states have been working together to harmonize sales tax collection and have created the Streamlined Sales and Use Tax Agreement (SSUTA). The SSUTA member states hope that Congress can be persuaded to allow them to require out-of-state vendors to collect taxes from customers in SSUTA member states.

In the 112th Congress, S. 1452 and H.R. 2701 (Senator Durbin and Representative Conyers) would grant SSUTA member states the authority to compel out-of-state vendors in other member states to collect sales and use taxes. In addition, H.R. 3179 (Representative Womack) would also grant states the authority to compel out-of-state vendors to collect use taxes provided selected simplification efforts are implemented.

A related issue is the "Internet Tax Moratorium." The relatively narrow moratorium prohibits (1) new taxes on Internet access services and (2) multiple or discriminatory taxes on Internet commerce. Congress has extended the "Internet Tax Moratorium" twice. The most recent extension expires November 1, 2014. The moratorium is distinct from the remote use tax collection issue, but has been linked in past debates. An analysis of the Internet tax moratorium is beyond the scope of this report.

This report will be updated as legislative events warrant.

Contents

Tables

Contacts

Introduction

State governments rely on general sales and use taxes for just under one-third (30.8%) of their total tax revenue—approximately $241 billion in FY2008. Local governments derive 11.6% of their tax revenue—approximately $63 billion in FY2008—from general sales and use taxes. Both state and local sales taxes are usually collected by vendors at the point of transaction and levied as a percentage of a product's retail price. Alternatively, use taxes, levied at the same rate, are often not collected by the vendor if the vendor does not have nexus (loosely defined as a physical presence) in the consumer's state. Consumers are required to remit use taxes to their taxing jurisdiction for the use of the product purchased. Compliance with this requirement, however, is quite low.

State and local governments are concerned that the expansion of e-commerce, which is estimated to reach approximately $3.9 trillion in 2011, is gradually eroding their tax base.[1] This concern arises in part because the U.S. Supreme Court ruled out-of-state vendors are not required to collect sales taxes for states in which they (the vendors) do not have nexus. In hopes of stemming the potential loss of tax revenue, several states are participating in an initiative to simplify and coordinate their tax codes—called the Streamlined Sales and Use Tax Agreement (SSUTA). The member states hope that Congress could be persuaded to allow them to require out-of-state vendors to collect taxes from resident customers.

Congress has a role in this issue because interstate commerce, in most cases, falls under the Commerce Clause of the Constitution. Congress will likely be asked to choose between taking either an active or passive role in the debate. In the 112th Congress, S. 1452 and H.R. 2701 (Senator Durbin and Representative Conyers) would grant SSUTA member states the authority to compel out-of-state vendors in other member states to collect sales and use taxes. On the House side, H.R. 3179 (Representative Womack) would also grant states the authority to compel out-of-state vendors to collect use taxes provided selected simplification efforts are implemented.

In the 111th Congress, H.R. 5660 (former Representative Delahunt) would have granted SSUTA member states the authority to compel out-of-state vendors to collect sales and use taxes. A more passive approach by Congress could involve states implementing the SSUTA without congressional approval. State enforcement of remote collection would likely face legal challenges, and the outcome of these legal challenges is uncertain. This report intends to clarify significant issues in the remote sales tax collection debate, beginning with a description of state and local sales and use taxes.

The impact of congressional action (or inaction) on the remote collection issue will vary significantly by state. For this reason, the report includes a state-by-state analysis of the sales tax.

---

[1] Donald Bruce, William F. Fox, LeAnn Luna, "State and Local Government Sales Tax Revenue Losses From Electronic Commerce," *State Tax Notes*, 52(7):537-558, May 18, 2009, p. 7. Version available at University of Tennessee Center for Business and Economic Research, http://cber.bus.utk.edu/ecomm.htm.

State and Local Sales and Use Taxes

In 1932, Mississippi was the first state to impose a general state sales tax. During the remainder of the 1930s, an era characterized by declining revenue from corporate and individual income taxes, 23 other states followed suit and implemented a general sales tax. At the time, the sales tax was relatively easy to administer and raised a significant amount of revenue despite a relatively low rate. Given the relative success of the sales tax in raising revenue, 45 states and the District of Columbia added the sales tax to their tax infrastructure by the late 1960s. The last of the 45 states to enact a general sales and use tax was Vermont in 1969.

Components of the Sales and Use Tax

The revenue generated by a sales and use tax, assuming a given level of compliance, depends on the base of the tax and the tax rate. States often have similar consumption items included in their tax base, but they are far from uniform. Tax rates can also vary considerably, depending on the state's reliance on other revenue sources. The SSUTA is intended to provide uniform definitions across states for items included in the base and the applicable tax rates. Following is an analysis of the variation of these components across the states.

Tax Base

The sales tax is perhaps better identified as a transaction tax on the transfer of tangible personal property, as expenditures on most services are typically excluded from the state sales tax base. In addition, in most states (34) and the District of Columbia, groceries are also exempt from state and local sales taxes or taxed at a lower rate.[2]

Table 1 presents the most recently available data on state and local tax revenue and an estimate of each state's sales tax base. The sales tax revenue includes collections from individuals as well as businesses. The estimate of the sales tax base as a share of income is a rough approximation of the state sales tax base.[3] A higher percentage likely indicates (1) a greater number of items and services subject to the sales and (2) greater compliance. In the case of Hawaii, where over 100% of personal income is includable in the tax base, the percentage likely measures some degree of pyramiding of the sales tax. Pyramiding occurs when a business pays sales tax on a good then collects more sales tax when the good is sold. Pyramiding is common in many other states, but is difficult to quantify. In total, roughly half of personal income is spent on items subject to the sales taxes.

---

[2] Federation of Tax Administrators, State Sales Tax Rates and Food and Drug Exemptions, January 1, 2011, available at http://www.taxadmin.org/fta/rate/sales.pdf. In three additional states, groceries are subject to local sales taxes only.

[3] A common identity in economics is: income = consumption + saving. The sales tax is a tax on consumption.

Table 1. State and Local Sales Taxes as Percentage of Total Personal Income, 2008

(amounts in thousands; tax data are FY2008)

State	Total State and Local Sales Taxes FY2008	State Sales Taxes FY2008	Local Sales Taxes FY2008	State Personal Income 2008	Sales Tax Base as Share of Income[a]
United States	$304,434,833	$241,007,659	$63,427,174	$12,380,225,000	49.5%
Alabama	4,148,232	2,287,288	1,860,944	158,696,556	43.2%
Alaska	214,647	—	214,647	30,562,542	—
Arizona	9,108,974	6,433,468	2,675,506	223,961,131	47.3%
Arkansas	3,715,891	2,807,943	907,948	93,480,735	63.2%
California	41,089,543	31,972,874	9,116,669	1,604,154,823	39.4%
Colorado	5,259,552	2,312,731	2,946,821	214,976,720	44.6%
Connecticut	3,545,734	3,545,734	—	200,363,527	40.9%
Delaware	—	—	—	35,614,625	—
Florida	22,852,595	21,518,100	1,334,495	739,403,128	55.7%
Georgia	9,770,932	5,796,653	3,974,279	342,934,981	51.7%
Hawaii	2,619,595	2,619,595	—	54,700,256	101.3%
Idaho	1,347,452	1,347,327	125	50,501,995	50.4%
Illinois	9,309,321	7,935,417	1,373,904	554,795,334	31.8%
Indiana	5,738,829	5,738,829	—	223,683,334	44.2%
Iowa	2,431,216	1,840,862	590,354	114,428,772	44.5%
Kansas	3,059,541	2,264,747	794,794	111,957,460	50.2%
Kentucky	2,875,836	2,875,836	—	138,485,619	46.1%
Louisiana	7,107,737	3,459,383	3,648,354	169,791,033	63.6%
Maine	1,060,557	1,060,557	—	48,296,992	48.4%
Maryland	3,748,933	3,748,933	—	274,285,685	34.7%
Massachusetts	4,098,089	4,098,089	—	333,814,725	29.3%
Michigan	8,225,599	8,225,599	—	353,140,341	50.1%
Minnesota	4,668,525	4,550,838	117,687	226,148,739	43.5%
Mississippi	3,135,390	3,135,390	—	90,346,843	55.6%
Missouri	5,055,423	3,228,274	1,827,149	219,694,892	46.8%
Montana	—	—	—	34,140,823	—
Nebraska	1,875,530	1,534,134	341,396	71,567,563	44.4%
Nevada	3,373,043	3,077,433	295,610	104,729,983	57.0%
New Hampshire[b]	—	—	—	57,793,463	—
New Jersey	8,915,515	8,915,515	—	447,988,666	28.8%
New Mexico	2,765,950	1,949,768	816,182	66,773,297	89.3%
New York	23,032,617	11,294,737	11,737,880	937,173,182	34.4%

State	Total State and Local Sales Taxes FY2008	State Sales Taxes FY2008	Local Sales Taxes FY2008	State Personal Income 2008	Sales Tax Base as Share of Income[a]
North Carolina	7,225,971	5,269,929	1,956,042	329,969,962	44.9%
North Dakota	622,166	530,078	92,088	26,591,382	52.9%
Ohio	9,523,835	7,865,674	1,658,161	414,458,285	39.1%
Oklahoma	3,611,865	2,096,220	1,515,645	134,504,737	67.4%
Oregon	—	—	—	139,306,268	—
Pennsylvania	9,190,350	8,873,309	317,041	508,248,855	32.6%
Rhode Island	846,870	846,870	—	44,060,770	28.2%
South Carolina	3,174,420	3,051,608	122,812	148,891,535	53.1%
South Dakota	1,003,308	732,438	270,870	31,710,437	68.8%
Tennessee[b]	8,793,990	6,832,948	1,961,042	219,160,305	52.3%
Texas	27,076,344	21,668,972	5,407,372	968,231,053	48.5%
Utah	2,612,849	1,964,119	648,730	88,792,239	60.7%
Vermont	344,402	338,941	5,461	24,459,780	40.3%
Virginia	4,736,329	3,656,789	1,079,540	348,265,469	42.3%
Washington	13,732,876	11,344,622	2,388,254	287,010,560	48.0%
West Virginia	1,109,822	1,109,822	—	57,207,827	48.5%
Wisconsin	4,567,730	4,268,068	299,662	213,316,800	46.3%
Wyoming	1,216,295	981,198	235,097	27,016,369	75.1%

Source: U.S. Bureau of Census, State and Local Government Finances by Level of Government and by State: 2007-08, available at http://www.census.gov/govs/estimate/.

Notes: States in italics are states without a broad based income tax.

a.   Mikesell, John, "Retail Sales Taxes, 1995-98: An Era Ends," *State Tax Notes*, February 21, 2000, p. 594. Data are for the 1998 tax year, the latest year for which estimates of sales tax base were made.

b.   New Hampshire and Tennessee levy a tax on income from dividends and interest.

Tax Rate

The second component of a sales tax is the tax rate applied to the base. In 34 states, local governments piggy-back a local sales tax (which often varies among localities within the state) on the state sales tax; 11 states and the District of Columbia levy a single rate (see **Table 2**), with no local taxes. Some states in the group of 34 may collect a uniform local tax along with the state tax and send the local revenue share back to the localities. This structure would look like a single rate to the consumer because vendors typically do not differentiate between the state and local share. For example, vendors in Virginia levy a 5.0% sales tax on purchases and remit the entire amount to the state. The state then returns what would have been raised by a 1.0% tax back to the local jurisdiction where the tax was collected. The state of Virginia keeps the remaining 4.0%.

As of January 1, 2011, California had the highest state sales tax rate of 7.25%. Indiana, Mississippi, New Jersey, Rhode Island, and Tennessee had state sales tax rate of 7.0%. The state rate is only part of the total rate; as noted earlier, most states also levy a local sales tax. As of January 1, 2011, Arizona had the highest potential combined state and local rate of 12.1%, with Alabama second at 12.0%.

Residents in high sales tax rate jurisdictions could benefit more from Internet purchases (and tax evasion) relative to those in low tax rate states. Recognizing this potential revenue loss, many high-rate states have stepped up efforts to inform consumers of their responsibility to pay use taxes on Internet and mail-order catalog purchases. As suggested earlier, states with high rates—and whose residents have a greater incentive to evade taxes—are exposed to greater potential revenue losses from the growth of Internet commerce. Because of the greater potential losses, these states are more likely to support reforms that help maintain their sales and use tax revenue base.

The tax base and tax rate determine how much revenue is generated by the sales tax for each jurisdiction. The share lost to non-compliance arising from e-commerce, however, varies considerably by state. Part of the variance can be attributed to the two components of the overall compliance: sales tax collected by vendors and use tax remitted by purchasers. Researchers on e-commerce estimated a relatively high vendor compliance though considerably lower purchaser compliance.[4]

Table 2 also lists each state's current status with the SSUTA. The "member" states (20) have all enacted laws that fully comply with the SSUTA. A second group of states (4) are considered "associate" states and not full members because relatively small technical changes are needed in state tax laws to be in full compliance with SSUTA. A third group of states (19) are participating in the streamlining effort but have not made the necessary uniformity changes in state sales tax law to be considered for member or associate status.

Table 2. SSUTA Status and State and Local Sales Tax Rates

State	SSUTA Status[a]	State Tax Rate[b]	Top Local Rate[b]	Maximum Combined	Rank
United States Average	—	5.047%	2.547%	7.594%	—
Alabama	Advisory	4.000%	8.000%	12.000%	2
Alaska	No Sales Tax	—	7.500%	7.500%	28
Arizona	Advisory	6.600%	5.500%	12.100%	1
Arkansas	Member	6.000%	5.500%	11.500%	3
California	Advisory	8.250%	3.000%	11.250%	5
Colorado	Non-Participant	2.900%	7.000%	9.900%	12
Connecticut	Advisory	6.000%	—	6.000%	38
Delaware	No Sales Tax	—	—	—	47
Florida	Advisory	6.000%	1.500%	7.500%	28
Georgia	Associate	4.000%	4.000%	8.000%	21

---

[4] Bruce, Donald, William F. Fox, LeAnn Luna, "State and Local Government Sales Tax Revenue Losses From Electronic Commerce," *State Tax Notes*, 52(7):537-558, May 18, 2009. Version available at University of Tennessee Center for Business and Economic Research, http://cber.bus.utk.edu/ecomm.htm.

State	SSUTA Status[a]	State Tax Rate[b]	Top Local Rate[b]	Maximum Combined	Rank
Hawaii	Advisory	4.000%	0.500%	4.500%	46
Idaho	Not Advisory	6.000%	3.000%	9.000%	15
Illinois	Advisory	6.250%	4.250%	10.500%	10
Indiana	Member	7.000%	—	7.000%	32
Iowa	Member	6.000%	2.000%	8.000%	21
Kansas	Member	6.300%	5.000%	11.300%	4
Kentucky	Member	6.000%	—	6.000%	38
Louisiana	Advisory	4.000%	6.750%	10.750%	8
Maine	Advisory	5.000%	—	5.000%	44
Maryland	Advisory	6.000%	—	6.000%	38
Massachusetts	Advisory	6.250%	—	6.250%	37
Michigan	Member	6.000%	—	6.000%	38
Minnesota	Member	6.875%	1.000%	7.875%	25
Mississippi	Advisory	7.000%	0.250%	7.250%	31
Missouri	Advisory	4.225%	6.625%	10.850%	6
Montana	No Sales Tax	—	—	—	47
Nebraska	Member	5.500%	2.000%	7.500%	28
Nevada	Member	6.850%	1.250%	8.100%	20
New Hampshire	No Sales Tax	—	—	—	47
New Jersey	Member	7.000%	—	7.000%	32
New Mexico	Advisory	5.125%	5.625%	10.750%	9
New York	Advisory	4.000%	5.000%	9.000%	15
North Carolina	Member	5.750%	3.000%	8.750%	18
North Dakota	Member	5.000%	2.500%	7.500%	27
Ohio	Associate	5.500%	2.250%	7.750%	26
Oklahoma	Member	4.500%	6.350%	10.850%	7
Oregon	No Sales Tax	—	—	—	47
Pennsylvania	Not Advisory	6.000%	2.000%	8.000%	21
Rhode Island	Member	7.000%	0.000%	7.000%	32
South Carolina	Advisory	6.000%	3.000%	9.000%	15
South Dakota	Member	4.000%	2.000%	6.000%	38
Tennessee	Associate	7.000%	2.750%	9.750%	13
Texas	Advisory	6.250%	2.000%	8.250%	19
Utah	Associate	4.700%	5.250%	9.950%	11
Vermont	Member	6.000%	1.000%	7.000%	35
Virginia	Advisory	4.000%	1.000%	5.000%	44

State	SSUTA Status[a]	State Tax Rate[b]	Top Local Rate[b]	Maximum Combined	Rank
Washington	Member	6.500%	3.000%	9.500%	14
West Virginia	Member	6.000%	—	6.000%	38
Wisconsin	Member	5.000%	1.500%	6.500%	36
Wyoming	Member	4.000%	4.000%	8.000%	21

Source: State and local sales tax rate data are from the Sales Tax Institute at http://www.salestaxinstitute.com/resources/rates. The highest combined rate and accompanying rank is a CRS calculation.

Notes: "Member" means full participant in SSUTA; "Associate" generally means technical changes need in state tax laws for state full conformity; "Advisory" means not conforming to SSTUA; "Not Advisory" means part of the project, but not advising decisions; and "Non-participating" means state is not working with other states toward conformity.

a. Status is as of January 1, 2011.

b. State and local sales tax rate data are as of May 1, 2011.

State Reliance on Sales Taxes

In addition to a sales tax, most states levy income taxes and almost every local jurisdiction (and some states) also levies a property tax. **Table 3** presents the relative reliance of each state and local government combined on the three principal revenue sources: sales taxes, income taxes, and property taxes. Reliance is measured as a percentage of total taxes collected. Other taxes include selective sales taxes such as motor fuels taxes, alcoholic beverages taxes, tobacco product taxes, and corporate income taxes.

The U.S. average reliance is greatest for the property tax at 30.8%, and the sales tax and individual income tax each accounted for 22.9% of tax revenue in FY2008. The top three states in sales tax reliance were Washington, Tennessee, and South Dakota. These three states do not levy a broad based income tax, thus increasing their reliance on sales taxes.[5]

Table 3. State and Local Government Sales Tax Reliance

(FY2008)

State	Total Taxes	Sales Tax Reliance Rank	General Sales Tax	Income Tax	Property Tax	Other Taxes
United States	$ 1,330,411,772		22.9%	22.9%	30.8%	23.4%
Alabama	14,040,755	14	29.5%	22.7%	16.4%	31.3%
Alaska	9,735,074	47	2.2%	0.0%	11.0%	86.8%
Arizona	22,992,377	4	39.6%	14.8%	29.2%	16.4%
Arkansas	9,405,740	6	39.5%	24.9%	15.5%	20.0%
California	186,014,884	25	22.1%	30.0%	28.4%	19.6%
Colorado	19,636,243	19	26.8%	25.8%	31.2%	16.2%

[5] New Hampshire and Tennessee levy a tax on income from dividends and interest.

State	Total Taxes	Sales Tax Reliance Rank	General Sales Tax	Income Tax	Property Tax	Other Taxes
Connecticut	23,115,325	42	15.3%	32.5%	36.0%	16.2%
Delaware	3,712,421	48	0.0%	28.7%	16.3%	55.1%
District of Columbia	5,397,980	40	16.6%	25.1%	32.0%	26.3%
Florida	73,351,398	13	31.2%	0.0%	41.3%	27.6%
Georgia	33,632,501	16	29.1%	26.3%	30.4%	14.3%
Hawaii	6,736,782	7	38.9%	22.9%	18.6%	19.6%
Idaho	4,939,722	18	27.3%	29.1%	23.9%	19.7%
Illinois	57,834,014	41	16.1%	17.8%	36.8%	29.2%
Indiana	22,954,400	22	25.0%	23.5%	30.2%	21.3%
Iowa	11,541,176	28	21.1%	25.4%	32.2%	21.3%
Kansas	11,877,315	20	25.8%	24.8%	31.0%	18.4%
Kentucky	14,156,697	30	20.3%	32.0%	19.6%	28.0%
Louisiana	17,950,501	5	39.6%	17.7%	15.8%	26.9%
Maine	5,932,772	34	17.9%	26.3%	36.4%	19.4%
Maryland	27,651,053	44	13.6%	40.4%	23.9%	22.1%
Massachusetts	33,997,340	45	12.1%	36.8%	34.3%	16.9%
Michigan	37,649,871	26	21.8%	20.3%	37.5%	20.3%
Minnesota	24,723,888	32	18.9%	31.5%	26.8%	22.8%
Mississippi	9,212,798	9	34.0%	16.8%	25.0%	24.2%
Missouri	19,872,542	21	25.4%	27.5%	27.6%	19.4%
Montana	3,448,016	48	0.0%	25.2%	34.1%	40.7%
Nebraska	7,508,042	23	25.0%	23.0%	33.1%	18.9%
Nevada	10,587,743	11	31.9%	0.0%	30.4%	37.8%
New Hampshire	4,962,804	48	0.0%	2.4%	61.6%	36.0%
New Jersey	53,790,897	39	16.6%	23.4%	42.2%	17.8%
New Mexico	7,746,740	8	35.7%	15.7%	14.5%	34.1%
New York	138,287,941	38	16.7%	33.6%	28.3%	21.5%
North Carolina	33,207,939	27	21.8%	33.1%	23.7%	21.4%
North Dakota	3,174,007	31	19.6%	10.0%	23.3%	47.1%
Ohio	46,660,185	29	20.4%	30.0%	29.1%	20.5%
Oklahoma	12,314,542	15	29.3%	22.6%	17.2%	30.9%
Oregon	12,531,550	48	0.0%	39.7%	34.0%	26.3%
Pennsylvania	54,109,616	37	17.0%	26.5%	28.7%	27.8%
Rhode Island	4,873,788	35	17.4%	22.4%	42.3%	17.9%
South Carolina	13,162,705	24	24.1%	21.8%	32.7%	21.5%
South Dakota	2,499,901	3	40.1%	0.0%	34.3%	25.5%

State	Total Taxes	Sales Tax Reliance Rank	General Sales Tax	Income Tax	Property Tax	Other Taxes
Tennessee	18,999,627	2	46.3%	1.5%	24.6%	27.6%
Texas	86,382,692	12	31.3%	0.0%	38.8%	29.8%
Utah	9,371,460	17	27.9%	27.7%	23.7%	20.8%
Vermont	2,935,601	46	11.7%	21.2%	40.1%	26.9%
Virginia	32,706,639	43	14.5%	30.9%	32.3%	22.3%
Washington	28,589,571	1	48.0%	0.0%	27.3%	24.7%
West Virginia	6,428,072	36	17.3%	23.6%	19.3%	39.9%
Wisconsin	24,372,341	33	18.7%	27.2%	36.2%	17.8%
Wyoming	3,693,784	10	32.9%	0.0%	34.1%	33.0%

Source: CRS calculations based on U.S. Bureau of Census, State and Local Government Finances by Level of Government and by State: 2007-08, available at http://www.census.gov/govs/estimate/.

Note: New Hampshire and Tennessee levy a tax on income from dividends and interest.

Description of the SSUTA

The entity that drafted the original Streamline Sales and Use Tax Agreement (SSUTA), the Streamlined Sales and Use Tax Project (SSTP), was created in 2000 by 43 states and the District of Columbia. These states and the District of Columbia wanted to simplify and better synchronize individual state sales and use tax laws. Its stated goal was to create a simplified sales tax system so all types of vendors—from traditional retailers to those conducting trade over the Internet— could easily collect and remit sales taxes. The member states believe that a simplified, relatively uniform tax code across states would make it easier for remote vendors to collect sales taxes on goods sold to out-of-state customers. The SSTP was dissolved once the SSUTA became effective on October 1, 2005. The latest amendments to the SSUTA were approved May 19, 2011.[6]

The SSUTA agreement explicitly identifies 10 points of focus.[7] Uniformity and simplification are the primary themes with state level administration of the sales and use tax a critical element in achieving the "streamlining" goal. The 10 points of focus can be condensed into four general requirements for simplification: (1) state level administration, (2) uniform tax base, (3) simplified tax rates, and (4) uniform sales sourcing rules. Each is discussed in more detail in the following sections.

State Level Administration

Administration of the sales tax for multistate businesses is complicated because state sales tax laws are not uniform.[8] Currently, multistate businesses file sales tax returns for each jurisdiction

---

[6] For the latest update, see http://www.streamlinedsalestax.org.

[7] SSUTA, Section 102: Fundamental Purpose, p. 7.

[8] For a discussion of the theoretical deficiencies U.S. sales and use tax administration, see Walter Hellerstein and Charles E. McLure Jr., "Sales Taxation of Electronic Commerce: What John Due Knew All Along," *State Tax Notes*, (continued...)

in which they are required to remit sales taxes. These state sales and use tax compliance rules are far from uniform, which increases compliance costs and the accompanying economic inefficiencies.

Under SSUTA, sales taxes would be remitted to a single state agency and businesses will no longer file tax returns with each state (and sometimes local jurisdiction) where they conduct business. States would bear some of the administrative cost of the technology employed to implement the new system.

States also would incur some additional administrative costs through vendor collection incentives. State and local governments currently compensate vendors for collection under a variety of rules and rates. Total vendor compensation would be somewhat standardized under SSUTA with three uniform brackets with rates set by each member state. SSUTA would require that rates decline as a business's tax collection volume increases. Total compensation for vendors in member states that require tax reporting by local jurisdiction is at least 0.75% of state and local sales and use tax collections. Total compensation for vendors in member states that *do not require* tax reporting by local jurisdiction is a minimum of 0.5% of sales and use tax collections.

As of this writing, 20 states were in full compliance with the terms of the SSUTA and are identified as "members." Another four states are "associate members." Only the member states will have taxes collected by remote vendors. **Table 2** lists the status of SSUTA adoption in each state.

Uniform Tax Base

As noted earlier, each state has established rules for what to include in the sales tax base, and definitions of these items are not uniform across states. The SSUTA includes a section requiring that within each state, all jurisdictions use the same tax base.[9] Thus, if the state excludes groceries from the sales tax, all local governments within the state must also exclude groceries. This seemingly straightforward requirement can become complicated. For example, as noted above, groceries are exempt from taxation in most states, whereas candy is taxable in several states. A common definition of candy (or food) must be agreed upon to implement a streamlined sales tax regime. Under SSUTA,

> "Candy" means a preparation of sugar, honey, or other natural or artificial sweeteners in combination with chocolate, fruits, nuts or other ingredients or flavorings in the form of bars, drops, or pieces. "Candy" shall not include any preparation containing flour and shall require no refrigeration.

Each state would retain the choice over whether the item is taxable (in the base) and the rate that applies to the product.

(...continued)

January 1, 2001, pp. 41-46.

[9] Streamlined Sales Tax Project, SSUTA, p. 13.

Simplified Tax Rates

In many states, local jurisdictions tax goods at different rates. This complication is mostly remedied under the SSUTA, as each state would be permitted only one state tax rate (with an exception for a second state rate on food and drugs). Each state can add one additional local jurisdiction rate, based on ZIP code. The member state must maintain a catalogue of rates for all ZIP codes. For ZIP codes with multiple rates, an average rate for that ZIP code would apply.

Standard Rate Sourcing Rules for Cross-Jurisdictional Sales

Sourcing rules for sales within a member state between local jurisdictions, the vendor would collect the sales tax at the rate applicable for the vendor location. This is identified as "origin" sourcing. For sales into a member state from an out-of-state vendor, the vendor levies a tax at the agreed upon statewide rate applicable in the destination state. This is identified as "destination" sourcing and is the general rule under the SSUTA.

There is some debate about the "sourcing" aspect of the SSUTA. The single statewide rate, which is set by each member state, would be a combined state and local rate. If the combined statewide rate is the state rate plus an average of local rates, it is possible that some consumers will pay a higher combined tax rate than is required. It has been proposed that the member states would be required to include a provision in the implementing legislation that would allow consumers that "overpay" to receive a credit for overpayments.

SSUTA Stakeholders

The SSUTA enjoys the support of the National Governors Association (NGA). The NGA has endorsed the SSUTA with hopes that the agreement will address the Supreme Court's concerns about the burden on interstate commerce of collecting remote taxes. The association believes that requiring remote vendors to collect sales and use taxes under a new, simplified system will survive legal challenges. The official statement of the NGA position on the efforts to streamline state and local taxes begins with the following:

> The National Governors Association supports state efforts to pursue, through negotiations, the courts, and federal legislation, provisions that would require remote, out-of-state vendors to collect sales and use taxes from their customers. Such action is necessary to restore fairness between local retail store purchases and remote sellers and to provide a means for the states to collect taxes that are owed under existing law. The rapid growth of the Internet and electronic commerce underscores the importance of maintaining equitable treatment among all sellers.[10]

The NGA support is shared by other state and local government organizations, including the National Conference of State Legislatures (NCSL), the Federation of Tax Administrators (FTA), and the Multistate Tax Commission (MTC).

---

[10] National Governor's Association, *Policy Position EDC-10: Streamlining State Sales Tax Systems*, February 28, 2011, effective through Winter Meetings 2013, available at http://www.nga.org/portal/site/nga/menuitem.b14a675ba7f89cf9e8ebb856a11010a0.

Support also comes from large retailers who must collect sales taxes and believe the current system provides an unfair advantage to Internet retailers who do not collect such taxes. Many large brick-and-mortar companies with a strong Internet presence generally comply with guidelines like those under SSUTA and generally collect taxes on remote sales. Several retailers, however, are taking the middle ground in this debate. They understand the states' desire to more efficiently collect sales tax revenue in a fair manner, but they ask for greater simplification and increased vendor compensation from the states for collecting state sales taxes.

Opponents of SSUTA legislation include state and local governments who feel the administrative obstacles to streamlined sales taxes are too costly to overcome and may actually exceed the potential revenue gain. These governments suggest that increased compliance with use tax laws may better be achieved through elevated consumer awareness and more enforcement activities. In addition, some business groups maintain that the collection requirement, even with streamlining, would still be too burdensome.

Also opposing SSUTA legislation are several anti-tax groups who see the SSUTA as a new tax burden rather than a simplification of the current tax system. Anti-tax groups also argue that states compete to attract businesses and customers through lower tax rates and that this competition is good for consumers.

Congressional and State Legislative Activity

Remote seller collection legislation at the federal level includes bills requiring SSUTA adoption and bills that are not conditioned on SSUTA approval. State efforts have taken two tracks: adopting SSUTA type legislation and/or implementing so-called Amazon laws. Following is a brief discussion of this activity.

SSUTA Legislation

In the 112th Congress, S. 1452 (and H.R. 2701) would grant SSUTA member states the authority to compel out-of-state vendors in member states to collect sales and use taxes. The legislation would have responded to the Supreme Court's recommendation in *Quill Corporation v. North Dakota* that Congress act, under the Commerce Clause, to clarify state sales tax collection rules. More specifically, the legislation would have allowed states that have fully adopted the SSUTA to collect sales taxes from sufficiently large businesses, even if those businesses do not have a nexus in the state. A "sufficiently large business" is left to the governing board of the SSUTA to define.

Under S. 1452, Congress would grant authority to states to compel out-of-state vendors to collect sales taxes, on the condition that 10 states comprising at least 20% of the total population of all states imposing a sales tax have implemented the SSUTA. The legislation also includes additional requirements for administering the new sales tax system after the SSUTA adoption threshold has been achieved. These requirements included, but were not limited to,

- a centralized, one-stop multi-state registration system;

- uniform definitions of products and product-based exemptions;

- single tax rate per taxing jurisdiction with a single additional rate for food and drugs;

- single, state-level administration of sales and use taxes;

- uniform rules for sourcing (i.e., the tax rate imposed is based on the origin or destination of the product);

- uniform procedures for certification of tax information service providers;

- uniform rules for filing returns and performing audits; and

- reasonable compensation for sellers collecting and remitting taxes.

The SSUTA generally includes these provisions, though some modifications to the SSUTA or the legislation may be necessary for enactment.

Under the SSUTA, member states request that remote sellers voluntarily collect sales taxes on items purchased by customers outside their home state. Vendors in participating states who voluntarily collect the sales tax would be offered amnesty for previously uncollected taxes. Participating states have agreed to share the administrative burden of collecting taxes to ease tax collection for sellers. The states' obligations under the SSUTA include the following requirements.

Business-to-business transactions are often exempt from the retail sales tax, particularly in cases where the purchaser is using the good as an input to production. These transactions are exempt because including the transactions could lead to the "pyramiding" of the sales tax. For example, if a coffee shop were to pay a retail sales tax on the purchase of coffee, and then impose a retail sales tax on coffee brewed for the final consumer, the total sales tax paid for the cup of coffee would likely exceed the statutory rate. Products that a business purchases for resale are typically not assessed a retail sales tax for a similar reason. If a coffee shop buys beans only for resale, levying a sales tax on the wholesale purchase of the beans and then on the retail sale would more than double the statutory rate. The tax treatment of business purchases is not uniform across states. According to some estimates, approximately 18% of business purchases are taxable depending on the state.

Many individuals and organizations are also exempt from state sales taxes. Entities wishing to claim the sales tax exemption are often issued a certificate indicating their tax-free status and are required to present this certification at the point of transaction. Non-profit organizations, such as those whose mission is religious, charitable, educational, or promoting public health, often hold sales tax-exempt status.

The SSUTA would establish a system in which states would use common definitions for goods and services. Once a uniform definition is established, states would then indicate whether the good or service is taxable. In addition, states would identify which entities would be exempt from paying sales taxes (e.g., non-profit or religious organizations).

Other Remote Seller Sales Tax Collection Legislation

In the 112th Congress, H.R. 3179, the Market Place Equity Act of 2011, introduced by Representative Womack, would attempt to achieve the same policy objective without a formal multistate compact like SSUTA. Instead, H.R. 3179 would authorize states to compel out-of-state vendors to collect sales and use taxes if the following requirements were satisfied:

- the state creates a remote seller sales and use tax return and requires filing no more frequently than in-state vendors;

- the state maintains a uniform tax base across the state;

- the state uses one of three structures for remote sales tax collection: (1) a single state and local "blended" rate, (2) a single maximum state rate exclusive of any additional local rates, or (3) the destination rate which would be the actual rate of the customer's jurisdiction.

In addition, a final condition requires that the rates determined in (1) and (2) above cannot exceed the average rate applicable to in-state vendors. For purposes of (3), the state must provide vendors access to a tax rate database for all jurisdictions. Remote vendors with total United States remote sales under $1 million or remote vendors with less than $100,000 in a given state, are exempt from collection responsibility.

Amazon Laws

Some states have begun to enact what are called "Amazon Laws." The "Amazon" modifier refers to the large Internet retailer that is located in Washington State. Amazon collects sales taxes only in the states where they claim their presence legally requires collection. In addition to Washington State, Amazon reportedly collects sales taxes in these additional states: Kansas, Kentucky, New York, and North Dakota.[11] At issue are affiliate agreements between Amazon and retailers that provide an Internet portal to Amazon. Typically, the affiliates are compensated for transactions that result from the so-called "click through" to Amazon.

New York State, the first to enact a so-called Amazon Law in 2008, claimed that the affiliate relationship constituted physical presence for Amazon.[12] Along with the physical presence established by the affiliate relationship came responsibility for collecting sales taxes on products sold to New York residents by Amazon. Several legal challenges to these so-called Amazon laws have been presented; a thorough legal analysis of these challenges extends beyond the scope of this report. Some proponents of the SSUTA see the growth of Amazon Laws as possibly complicating simplification efforts.

Economic Issues

During the debate about so-called "streamlining" legislation, there are several economic issues Congress may consider: (1) How will the SSUTA influence the economic efficiency and equity of state tax systems? (2) What will be the impact of changes in the treatment of Internet transactions on states that are more reliant on the sales tax? (3) What will the potential revenue loss be, absent changes in the treatment of Internet transactions? A summary of these issues follows.

---

[11] The American Independent Business Alliance, an advocacy group supporting the collection of sales taxes on Amazon sales, identified these states. The information is available at http://www.amiba.net/resources/news-archive/amazon-nexus-subsidiaries.

[12] Other states with an "Amazon Law" include Illinois, Rhode Island, and North Carolina. For more see Steele, Thomas H., Andres Vallejo, and Kirsten Wolff, "No Solicitations: The 'Amazon' Laws And the Perils of Affiliate Advertising," *State Tax Notes*, March 28, 2011, pp. 939- 944.

Efficiency

A commonly held view among economists is that a "good" tax (or more precisely, an efficient tax) minimizes distortions in consumer behavior. Broadly speaking, economists maintain that individuals should make the same choices before and after a tax is imposed. The greater the distortions in behavior caused by a tax, the greater the economic welfare loss. A sales tax levied on all consumer expenditures equally would satisfy this definition of efficiency. As noted earlier, however, under the current state sales tax system, all consumption expenditures are not treated equally. The growth of tax-free Internet transactions, both business-to-business and business-to-consumer, will likely amplify the efficiency losses from altered consumer behavior.

An alternative theory concerning economic efficiency in sales taxation is referred to as "optimal commodity taxation." Under an optimal commodity tax, the tax rate is based on (or determined by) what is termed the price elasticity of demand for the product (sometimes called the "Ramsey Rule"). Products that are price inelastic, meaning quantity demanded is unresponsive to changes in price, should be levied a higher rate of tax. In contrast, products that are price elastic should have a lower rate of tax. If products purchased over the Internet are relatively more price elastic, then the lower tax rate created by effectively tax-free Internet transactions may improve economic efficiency as behavioral changes are reduced. However, the price elasticity of products available over the Internet is difficult to measure and the efficiency gain, if any, is suspected to be small.

An additional economic inefficiency arises if vendors change location to avoid collecting sales taxes. The location change would likely result in higher transportation costs. In the long run, it is conceivable that the higher transportation costs would erode the advantage of evading the sales tax.

For example, consider a Virginia consumer who wants to buy a set of woodworking chisels. The local Virginia hardware store sells the set for $50 (including profit). An Internet-savvy hardware store in Georgia is willing to sell the same chisel set for $52 inclusive of profit and shipping costs. So, before taxes, the local retailer could offer the chisels at a lower price. The marginal customer, who is indifferent between the two retailers before taxes (even though the Internet is more expensive, it is more convenient), is therefore just as likely to buy from the Internet retailer as from the local retailer.

Virginia imposes a state and local sales tax of 5.0%, thus yielding a final sales price to the consumer of $52.50. Given the higher relative price inclusive of the tax, the marginal consumer, along with many other consumers, would likely switch to buying chisels from the Georgia-based Internet retailer (assuming these consumers do not feel compelled to pay the required Virginia use tax on the Internet purchase). The diversion from retail to the Internet in response to the non-collection of the use tax represents a loss in economic efficiency. The additional $2 in production costs ($52 less $50) represents the efficiency loss to society from evading the use tax.

Note that in the absence of sales and use taxes, the Internet vendor in the above example may yield to market forces and close up shop. However, if the Internet vendor continues to operate even without the tax advantage, it could be the case that consumers are willing to pay higher prices for the convenience of Internet shopping. If this were true, then the higher "production costs" for Internet vendors would not necessarily result in an efficiency loss.

Equity

The sales tax is often criticized as a regressive tax—a tax that disproportionately burdens the poor. Assuming Internet shoppers are relatively better off and do not remit use taxes as prescribed by state law, they can avoid paying tax on a larger portion of their consumption expenditures than those without Internet access at home or work. Consumers without ready Internet access are not afforded the same opportunity to "evade" the sales and use tax. In this way, electronic commerce may arguably exacerbate the regressiveness of the sales tax, at least in the short run. As computers and access to the Internet become more readily available, the potential inequity arising from this aspect of the "digital divide" could diminish.

Equity issues also arise with respect to businesses. Currently, local retailers are required to collect sales taxes for the state at the point of sale. Internet retailers, in contrast, are not faced with that administrative burden. Thus, two otherwise equal retailers face different state and local tax burdens. In relatively high tax rate states, this disparity may be significant. As noted earlier, consumers in these high tax rate states have a greater incentive to purchase from out-of-state vendors, exacerbating the tax burden differential.

Differential Effect Among States

The growth of Internet-based commerce will have the greatest effect on the states most reliant on the sales and use tax. In addition to having more revenue at risk, high reliance states also face greater efficiency losses because of their generally higher state tax rates. As noted above, higher rates drive a larger wedge between the retail price inclusive of the sales tax and the Internet price and thus exacerbate the efficiency loss from the sales tax. States with low rates (and less reliance) would tend to have a smaller wedge between the two modes of transaction. States with both a high rate and high reliance would tend to recognize the greatest revenue loss from a ban on the taxation of Internet transactions.

Revenue Loss Estimates

Researchers estimated in April 2009 that total state and local revenue loss from "new e-commerce" in 2011 will be approximately $10.1 billion.[13] "New e-commerce" is the lost revenue from states not collecting the use tax on remote Internet transactions. This estimate excludes purchases made over the telephone or through catalogs that would have occurred anyway. California is projected to lose $1.7 billion; Texas, $774 million; and New York, $770 million.

---

[13] Bruce, Donald, William F. Fox, and LeAnn Luna, "State and Local Government Sales Tax Revenue Losses from Electronic Commerce," *State Tax Notes*, 52(7):537-558, May 18, 2009. Version available at University of Tennessee Center for Business and Economic Research, http://cber.bus.utk.edu/ecomm.htm.

Author Contact Information

Steven Maguire
Specialist in Public Finance
smaguire@crs.loc.gov, 7-7841